PEGASUS ENCYCLOPEDIA LIBRARY

Food and Nutrition
DISEASES AND ILLNESS

Edited by: Pallabi B. Tomar, Hitesh Iplani
Managing editor: Tapasi De
Designed by: Vijesh Chahal, Anil Kumar, Rohit Kumar
Illustrated by: Suman S. Roy, Tanoy Choudhury
Colouring done by: Vinay Kumar, Kiran Kumari & Pradeep Kumar

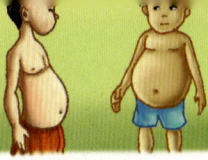

CONTENTS

Introduction 3

What is a disease? 4

What is illness? 6

Nutritional deficiency diseases 7

Types of illness 10

Types of nutritional deficiency diseases explained 12

Protein energy malnutrition 27

Prevention and management 29

Test Your Memory 31

Index 32

Introduction

Diseases are one of the factors threatening us from having a properly functional life. Throughout our history, epidemics have caused the extinction of whole populations. Over the last century, man has discovered many micro-organisms that cause diseases in humans and animals, and has learned how to protect himself from them, by either prevention or treatment.

Diseases and illness are any disturbance or irregularity in the normal functioning of the body that probably has a specific cause and identifiable symptoms.

The terms illness and disease are heard on a regular basis. Illness and disease both cause the same feelings of discomfort, pain or unease in people. However, an illness is more of a subjective feeling. This means that there is really no identifiable reason behind the condition. Of course, if the condition behind the illness is identified, it is more often referred to as a disease. However, in more generalized terms, we can define an illness as a state where the person has feelings of pain or discomfort that does not have an identifiable reason.

Astonishing fact

Over 90 per cent of diseases are caused or complicated by stress.

What is a disease?

A disease is any abnormal condition of the body or mind that causes discomfort, dysfunction or distress to the person affected or those in contact with the person. Sometimes the term is used broadly to include injuries, disabilities, syndromes, symptoms, deviant behaviours while in other contexts these maybe considered distinguishable categories.

Pathology is the study of diseases. The subject of systematic classification of diseases is referred to as **Nosology**. The broader body of knowledge about diseases and their treatments is **Medicine**.

The oldest known disease in the world is leprosy.

What is a disease?

What we call a disease, is our body's reaction to something that interferes with its normal functioning. An organ remains ill and is eventually destroyed, as long as the source of interference is not removed. A malfunctioning organ can negatively influence other organs and systems (circulatory, nervous, lymphatic) cooperating with it. There is constant struggle between health and illness in the life of our body. We could not stay alive without this struggle.

Disease is the defensive reaction of our body's mechanisms designed to keep us healthy. We all have these mechanisms. They are necessary to remove disorders in the way our body functions. They also give us warning signals when these disorders begin. To stay healthy, we need to listen and understand what our body is trying to communicate to us. Do not treat diseases as your worst enemy. In a sense, they force us to make the first step on the way towards a healthy lifestyle.

Astonishing fact

Each year in America there are about 300,000 deaths that can be attributed to obesity.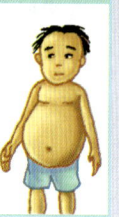

Some diseases, such as influenza are contagious or infectious, and can be transmitted by any of a variety of mechanisms, including droplets from coughs and sneezes, by bites of insects or other vectors, from contaminated water or food, etc.

Other diseases, such as cancer and heart disease are not considered to be due to infection, although micro-organisms may play a role.

DISEASES & ILLNESS

What is illness?

Illness and disease are not necessarily the same. Most people who have a disease will feel they have an illness, while others will feel perfectly healthy. A third group may claim to have an illness although they do not actually have a disease.

> A person afflicted with hexadectylism has six fingers or six toes on one or both hands and feet.

Illness, although often used to mean disease, can also refer to a person's perception of their health, regardless of whether they have a disease or not. A person without any disease may feel unhealthy and believe he has an illness. Another person may feel healthy and believe he does not have an illness even though he may have dangerously high blood pressure which may lead to a fatal heart attack or stroke!

Illness can be a synonymous with disease or it can be a person's perception of having poor health. Disease is an actual physical process which can cause an abnormal condition of the body or mind.

Nutritional deficiency diseases

Nutritional deficiency diseases occur when there is an absence of nutrients which are essential for growth and health. Lack of food leading to either malnutrition or starvation gives rise to these diseases. Another cause for a deficiency disease maybe due to a structural or biological imbalance in the individual's metabolic system.

There are more than 50 known **nutrients** in food. Nutrients enable body tissues to grow and maintain themselves. They contribute to the energy requirements of the individual organism and regulate the processes of the body. Carbohydrates, fats and proteins provide the body with energy. The energy producing component of food is measured in calories. Beside the water and fibre content of foods which are also important for their role in nutrition, the nutrients that serve functions other

> It takes about three hours for food to be broken down in the human stomach.

than energy production can be classified into four different groups— vitamins, fats, proteins and minerals. All are necessary for proper body function and survival.

There are about 25 mineral elements in the body usually appearing in the form of simple salts. Those which appear in large amounts are called macro minerals while those that are in small or trace amounts are micro minerals. Some that are essential are calcium, phosphorous, cobalt, copper, fluorine, iodine, iron, sodium, chromium and tin.

DISEASES & ILLNESS

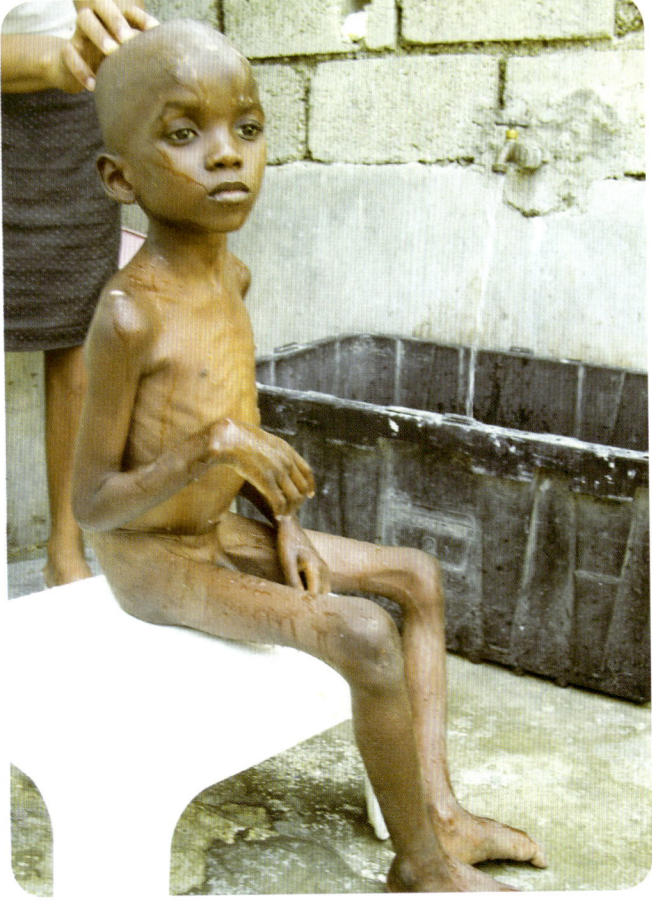

Nutritional deficiencies lead to a variety of health problems, the most prevalent of which are anaemia, beriberi, osteoporosis, pellagra and rickets. Anaemia occurs when the body does not have enough red blood cells to transport oxygen from the lungs to the body's cells. The most common symptom of anaemia is a constant feeling of fatigue. Making sure that one's diet contains the proper amounts of iron, folate and Vitamin B12 can prevent anaemia.

Nutritional deficiencies occur when the body lacks essential nutrients that are obtained from food. In developing countries, such dietary deficiencies are usually the result of poverty and insufficient food supplies. In the developed world, nutritional deficiencies are caused mainly by disorders that limit the body's intake or absorption of nutrients or to unhealthy eating or self-imposed dietary restrictions.

Nutritional deficiencies occur when a person's nutrient intake consistently falls below the recommended requirement. Children between 10–19 years of age face serious nutritional deficiencies worldwide, according to the World Health Organization. About 1,200 million or 19 per cent of adolescents suffer from poor nutrition that hurts their development and growth.

Astonishing fact

Native Americans used to use pumpkin seeds instead of medicine.

Nutritional deficiency diseases

Astonishing fact
It has been medically been proven that laughter is an effective pain killer.

Nutritional deficiency is a state where there are insufficient nutrients present for the body to function normally. Nutritional deficiency can affect one or more bodily functions and vary greatly in severity. Being deficient in a particular nutrient can cause the body to behave in a number of abnormal ways. For example, deficiency in calcium and phosphorus may cause problems for bone structure, nails and hair, whereas being deficient in protein will affect muscle and energy levels.

There are two main types of nutritional deficiencies— a general deficiency of calories and nutrients and a deficiency of specific nutrients. A general lack of nutrition maybe caused by poor eating as a result of severe illness or surgery. It may also be due to extreme dieting, general bad eating habits or deliberate starvation. Symptoms of a general deficiency may include weight loss, muscle weakness, tiredness, as well as skin and hair disorders.

Specific nutritional deficiencies may occur if people limit their diets because of certain beliefs. Specific nutritional deficiencies may result in a variety of disorders. These include iron deficiency like anaemia and the bone disorders like osteomalacia and rickets caused by a lack of calcium or Vitamin D. Vegetarians who fail to eat a balanced diet may often suffer from a lack of iron and other micronutrients. Vegetarians will suffer from a deficiency of Vitamin B12 if they do not eat B12 fortified foods.

DISEASES & ILLNESS

Types of illness

Physical

Conditions of the body or mind that cause pain, dysfunction or distress to the person affected or those in contact with the person can be deemed an illness. Sometimes the term is used broadly to include injuries, disabilities, syndromes, infections, symptoms, deviant behaviours. A pathogen or infectious agent is a biological agent that causes disease or illness to its host. A passenger virus is a virus that simply hitchhikes in the body of a person or infects the body without causing symptoms, illness or disease. Food borne illness or food poisoning is any illness resulting from the consumption of food contaminated with pathogenic bacteria, toxins, viruses or parasites.

> 3000 children die every day in Africa because of malaria.

Mental

Mental illnesses are medical conditions that disrupt a person's thinking, feeling, mood, ability to relate to others and daily functioning. Just as diabetes is a disorder of the pancreas, mental illnesses are medical conditions that often result in a lessened capacity for coping with the ordinary demands of life.

Serious mental illnesses include major depression, schizophrenia, bipolar disorder, obsessive compulsive disorder (OCD), panic disorder, post traumatic stress disorder (PTSD) and borderline personality disorder. The good news about mental illness is that recovery is possible.

Mental illnesses can affect persons of any age, race, religion or income. Mental illnesses are not the result of personal weakness, lack of character or poor upbringing. Mental illnesses are treatable. Most people diagnosed with a serious mental illness can experience relief from their symptoms by actively participating in an individual treatment plan.

> **Vitamin A was given the first letter of the alphabet, as it was the first to be discovered.**

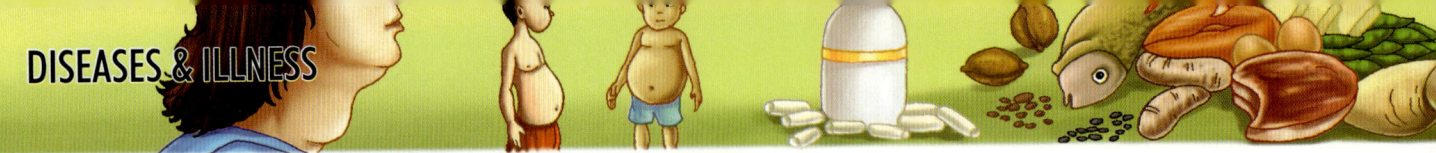

DISEASES & ILLNESS

Types of nutritional deficiency diseases explained

Vitamin A

Functions

Vitamin A is a fat-soluble organic compound that the body needs to remain healthy. Humans cannot make Vitamin A, so they must get it from foods in their diet. Vitamin A is sometimes called **retinol**.

Vitamin A affects many different systems of the body. It is especially important to maintaining good vision, a healthy immune system and strong bones. Vitamin A also helps turn on and off certain genes (gene expression) during cell division and differentiation. Getting the correct amount—not too little and not too much—of Vitamin A is essential for health. People who get too little Vitamin

> The purpose of tonsils is to destroy foreign substances that are swallowed or breathed in.

A have vision defects, are more likely to have damaged cells in the lining of body cavities and are more susceptible to infection. People who get too much Vitamin A have weakened bones that tend to break easily and have a chronic feeling of illness that includes headache, nausea, irritability, fatigue and muscle and joint pain. Excess Vitamin A can also cause birth defects in a developing foetus.

Types of nutritional deficiency diseases explained

Food sources

Vitamin A occurs in nature in two forms—preformed Vitamin A and proVitamin A, or carotene. Sources of Vitamin A can be divided into two groups— one is animal source and the other is vegetable source. Vitamin A comes from animal sources such as eggs and meat. Vitamin A in the form of retinyl palmitate, is found in beef, calf, chicken liver, eggs and fish liver oils as well as dairy products including whole milk, whole milk yogurt, whole milk cottage cheese, butter and cheese. The vegetable sources of beta-carotene are fat and cholesterol free. The body regulates the conversion of beta-carotene to Vitamin A, based on the body's needs. Sources of beta-carotene are carrots, pumpkin, sweet potatoes, winter squashes, cantaloupe, pink grapefruit, apricots, broccoli, spinach and most dark green, leafy vegetables.

Diseases

- A deficiency of Vitamin A may lead to eye problems with dryness of the conjunctiva and cornea, dry skin and hair, night blindness as well as poor growth.

- The eyes are obvious indicators of Vitamin A deficiency. One of the first symptoms is night blindness.

- Other indicators of Vitamin A deficiency include susceptibility to colds, flu, bacterial and viral infections, especially of the respiratory and urinary tract.

Astonishing fact

Teenagers are 50 per cent more vulnerable to colds than people over fifty.

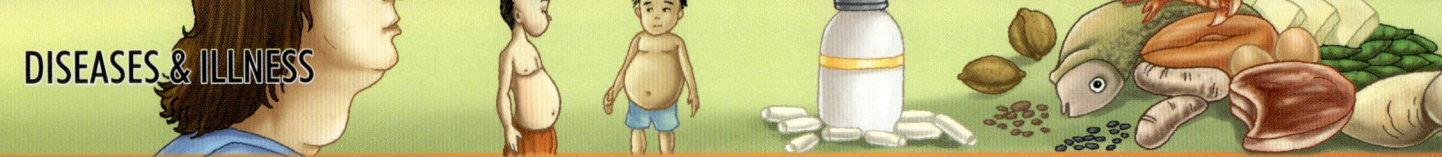

DISEASES & ILLNESS

Astonishing fact

Diabetes was the third leading cause of death by disease in America. It has increased by 50 per cent since 1965, and today affects at least 15 million people.

Vitamin D

Functions

It is a fat soluble vitamin that is found in food and can also be made in your body after exposure to ultraviolet rays from the sun. Vitamin D performs many vital functions in the body. It is required for the development of strong teeth and bones and maintains their structure. Vitamin D is essential for the healthy functioning of the parathyroid gland which regulates the levels of calcium in the body. Secondly, it maintains the balance between the calcium in the blood and the calcium in the bones. Next, Vitamin D helps in the absorption of calcium, phosphate and other minerals.

Finally, it regulates the excretion of calcium and phosphate by the kidneys.

Vitamin D has many therapeutic uses. Since it increases the absorption of calcium and regulates the deposition of minerals in the teeth and bones, it is used to treat arthritis and repair bones. Moreover, it is beneficial in cases of lowered immunity, chronic fatigue and even depression. It has been found that Vitamin D made in the presence of sunlight slows down the growth of cancer, and prevents degenerative diseases like heart diseases, blood pressure and muscular weakness.

Types of nutritional deficiency diseases explained

Food sources

As we know, the main source of Vitamin D comes from exposure to the sun's UVB rays but besides this, it is can also be found in various food items like fish (herring, mackerel, salmon, and sardines), egg yolks, orange juice, breakfast cereals, green leafy vegetables, fish liver oils, yogurt, cheese, etc. Fortified foods are other common sources of Vitamin D. In fact, one cup of Vitamin D fortified milk provides one-half of the recommended daily intakes for people between the ages of 19 and 50.

Nowadays, there are many multivitamins, calcium and Vitamin D supplements available to maintain Vitamin D concentration in the body and to overcome its deficiency. However, before taking any Vitamin D supplement, do consult your doctor as just like Vitamin D deficiency can lead to various health problems; its excess can also cause adverse effects on the body.

Diseases

Deficiency of Vitamin D has serious consequences, including retarded growth, defective teeth and dental caries. Moreover, its deficiency prevents assimilation of other minerals, and causes lowered immunity and premature aging. Since a shortage of Vitamin D leads to a reduction of calcium and phosphate, the bone formation is affected, leading to rickets in children and osteoporosis and conditions related to weak bones in adults. Other symptoms include muscular weakness, cramps, reduced energy and even convulsions.

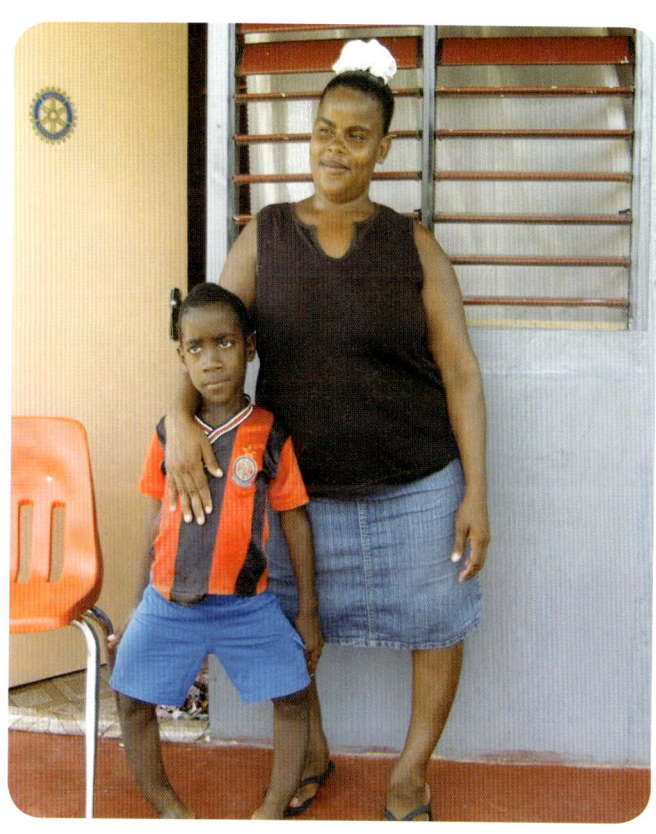

Astonishing fact

In 1918 and 1919 a world epidemic of simple Influenza killed 20 million people in the United States and Europe.

DISEASES & ILLNESS

Vitamin B complex

Functions

The Vitamin B complex consists of eight water soluble vitamins. It is present in the form of Vitamins B1, B2, B3, B5, B6, B12, folic acid and biotin. The B vitamins work together to boost metabolism, enhance the immune system and nervous system, keep the skin and muscles healthy, encourage cell growth and division and other benefits to your body. The main functions of this vitamin includes:

1. **B1/Thiamine**

   Breaks down carbohydrates to release energy; helps in normal functioning of the nervous system; helps to maintain the acidity level in the stomach and keeps the appetite normal.

2. **B3/Niacin**

   Helps to release energy from food, keeps the skin, mouth and digestive tract healthy. It is also vital for healthy mental functioning, helps to promote blood circulation and maintains the blood pressure.

3. **B2/Riboflavin**

   This helps to convert proteins, fats and carbohydrates into energy and is integral in maintaining healthy skin and eyes.

4. **B5/ Pantothenic acid**

   This helps in releasing energy from food, maintains normal functioning of the adrenal gland and aids formations of antibodies.

5. **B6/ Pyridoxine**

   This is required for protein metabolism, fluid balance and healthy maintenance of red blood cells.

6. **B12**

   This vitamin helps in red blood cell production and maintenance of healthy red blood cells. Deficiency of this vitamin can make people mentally lethargic, can cause shivering in the body and causes anaemia.

7. **Folic acid**

   Essential for growth and reproduction of red blood cells

8. **Biotin**

   Keeps the skin and hair healthy

Astonishing fact

One cannot catch cold at the North Pole in winter; neither can one contract the flu, nor most of the ailments transmitted viruses and germs. The winter temperature is so low in this part of the world that none of the standard disease causing micro-organisms can survive.

Types of nutritional deficiency diseases explained

Food sources

- B1 and B2 are found in cereals and whole grains. B1 is also found in potatoes, pork, seafood, liver and kidney beans. B2 is found in enriched bread, dairy products, liver and green leafy vegetables.

- B3 is found in liver, fish, chicken, lean red meat, nuts, whole grains and dried beans.

- B5 is found in almost all foods.

- B6 is found in fish, liver, pork, chicken, potatoes, wheat germ, bananas and dried beans.

- B7 is made by intestinal bacteria and is also in peanuts, liver, egg yolks, bananas, mushrooms, watermelon and grapefruit.

- B9 is in green leafy vegetables, liver, citrus fruits, mushrooms, nuts, peas, dried beans and wheat bread.

- B12 is found in eggs, meat, poultry, shellfish, milk and milk products.

17

DISEASES & ILLNESS

Diseases

Several deficiency diseases may result from the lack of B-vitamins. These include:

Vitamin	Disease
Vitamin B1	Deficiency causes beriberi, weight loss, emotional disturbances, swelling of bodily tissues, amnesia.
Vitamin B2 (Riboflavin)	Deficiency causes cracks in the lips, high sensitivity to sunlight, inflammation of the tongue, syphilis.
Vitamin B3 (Niacin)	Deficiency causes pellagra, mental confusion and even death.
Vitamin B6	Deficiency may lead to anaemia, dermatitis, high blood pressure.
Vitamin B7	Deficiency may lead to impaired growth and neurological disorders in infants.
Folic acid	Deficiency in pregnant women can lead to birth defects.
Vitamin B12	Deficiency causes pernicious anaemia, memory loss and other cognitive diseases.

Astonishing fact

A popular superstition is that if you put a piece of bread in a baby's crib, it will keep away diseases!

Vitamin C

Functions

Vitamin C is a water-soluble, antioxidant vitamin, also known as ascorbic acid. Vitamin C helps in the absorption of iron and maintains capillaries, bones and teeth. Humans do not have the ability to make their own Vitamin C. Therefore, we must obtain Vitamin C through our diet.

Vitamin C benefits us a lot. The best benefit offered by Vitamin C is collagen formation. Collagen is essentially a protein substance that helps keeping all the cells together. Vitamin C aids in the formation of collagen. Without Vitamin C, the formation of collagen is interrupted. Vitamin C is present and active within the cell wall where it aids in modifying pro-collagen into collagen.

Vitamin C helps in the absorption of iron as previously mentioned. Iron is essential to keep us healthy and vibrant. It maintains a healthy and clear skin, fresh complexion and healthy gums and teeth. It offers a healthy functioning for all glands and organs including adrenal and thyroid glands. It also aids in relieving all sort of stressors, both physical and psychological.

> **Asthma affects one in fifteen children under the age of eighteen.**

Food sources

Vitamin C is obtained from fruits and vegetables. Some excellent sources of Vitamin C are oranges, green peppers, watermelon, papaya, grapefruit, cantaloupe, strawberries, kiwi, mango, broccoli, tomatoes, Brussels sprouts, cauliflower, cabbage and citrus juices or juices fortified with Vitamin C.

Vitamin C is sensitive to light, air, and heat, so it is best to eat fruits and vegetables raw or minimally cooked in order to retain their full Vitamin C content.

Diseases

Scurvy is the main disease that is caused by the deficiency of Vitamin C, which is characterized by easily bruised skin, muscle fatigue, soft swollen gums, decreased wound healing and haemorrhaging, osteoporosis and anaemia. The primary cause of Vitamin C deficiency is poor diet. Vitamin C deficiency may develop in people who eat only such foods as dried meat, tea, toast and canned vegetables. Pregnancy, breastfeeding, surgery, and burns can significantly increase the body's requirements for Vitamin C and the risk of Vitamin C deficiency.

The symptoms of the deficiency of Vitamin C may include irritability, depression, weight loss, fatigue and general weakness. The gums become swollen, purple and spongy. The teeth eventually loosen. Infections may develop and wounds do not heal.

Calcium

Functions

Calcium plays an important role in the maintenance of health. It has been called the prime instigator of vital activity.

- This mineral is essential for the proper development of bones and teeth.

- It is necessary for the normal action of the heart and all muscle activity.

- It aids the clotting process of the blood and stimulates enzymes in the digestive process.

- Calcium is required for proper foetal growth, for normal health of the mother during pregnancy and lactation and for the secretion of breast milk.

- It speeds all the healing processes and controls the conduction mechanism in the nerve tissues so that messages travel fast enough for the functioning of the body.

- It is essential for proper utilization of phosphorus and Vitamin D, Vitamin A and Vitamin C.

Milk

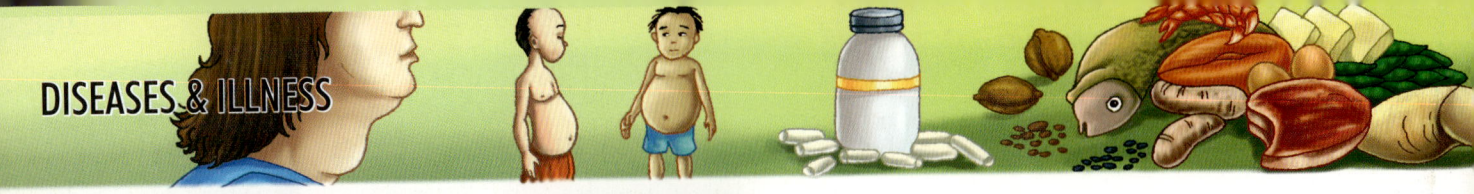

DISEASES & ILLNESS

Food sources

Milk and milk products such as non-fat cheese, cottage cheese and yogurt are sources of calcium. Other sources of calcium include dark green leafy vegetables, spinach, kale, turnip greens, cabbage, collard, mustard, seaweeds, alfalfa, broccoli, canned fish (especially sardines, clams, oysters and salmon) with bones and cooked dried beans and peas.

Diseases

Some of the indications of calcium deficiencies include skeletal abnormalities, such as osteopenia, osteomalacia, osteoporosis and rickets.

> **Red blood cells are created inside the marrow of your bones. They serve the important role of carrying blood around your body.**

Osteomalacia is a failure to mineralize the bone matrix, resulting in a reduction of the mineral content of the bone. In children, osteomalacia is known as rickets. When children have rickets, their bones become soft and flexible, bending in ways normal bones would not.

Osteopenia is the presence of less than normal amount of bone. Osteopenia, if not treated, may result in osteoporosis.

Osteoporosis occurs when the composition of the bone is normal, but the mass is so reduced that the skeleton loses its strength and becomes unable to perform its supporting role in the body. In this case, fractures may occur due to minor falls and bumps, or bones may even break under their own weight. People with osteoporosis may have a hump in their backs, scoliosis (curvature of the spine), kyphosis (rounded shoulders) or lose height. These conditions maybe caused by the buckling of their weakened spines, no longer being strong enough to hold the body upright.

The bones act as a reservoir for calcium. When the amount of calcium in the blood supply dips too low, calcium is borrowed from the bones. It is returned to the bones from calcium supplied through the diet. When diets are low in the mineral, there may not be sufficient amounts available to be returned to the bones. Over time, this net loss can lead to osteopenia or osteoporosis.

Types of nutritional deficiency diseases explained

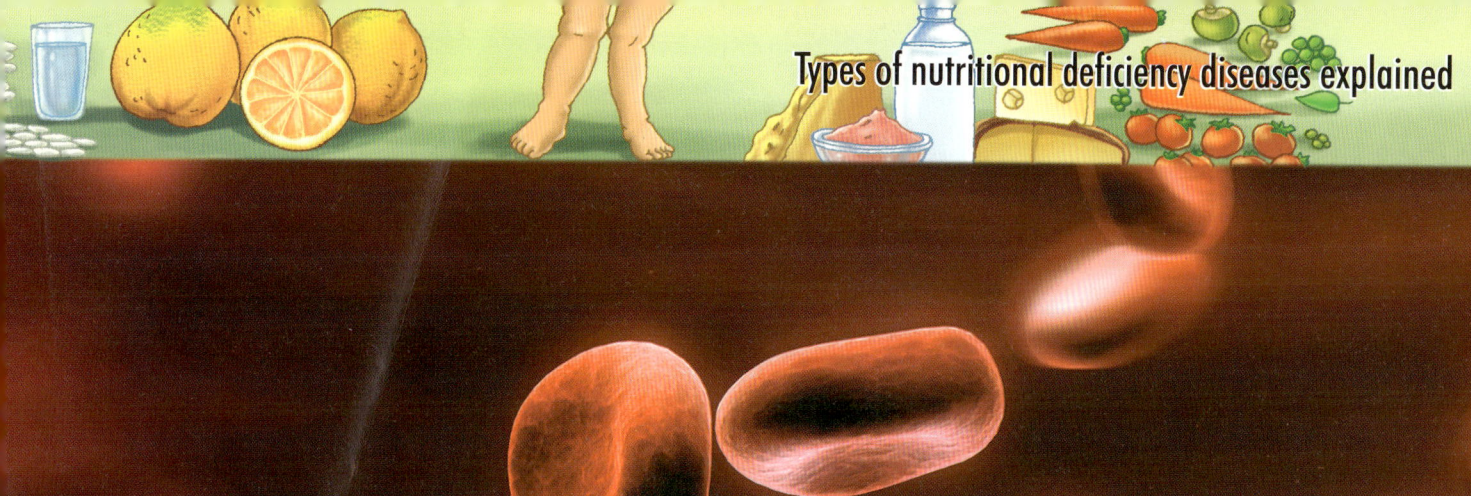

Iron

Functions

Iron is vital to the health of the human body and is found in every human cell, primarily linked with protein to form the oxygen-carrying molecule haemoglobin. The human body contains approximately 4 grams of iron.

Iron serves as the core of the haemoglobin molecule, which is the oxygen-carrying component of the red blood cell. Red blood cells pick up oxygen from the lungs and distribute the oxygen to the tissues throughout the body. The ability of red blood cells to carry oxygen is attributed to the presence of iron in the haemoglobin molecule.

If we lack iron, we will produce less haemoglobin, and therefore supply less oxygen to our tissues. Iron is also an important constituent of another protein called **myoglobin**. Myoglobin, like haemoglobin, is an oxygen-carrying molecule, which distributes oxygen to muscles cells, especially to skeletal muscles and to the heart.

Astonishing fact

Around 7 million people die every year from food poisoning out of a total of around 70 million cases. Careful food preparation and storage is vital in order to avoid dangerous toxins, viruses and bacteria.

23

DISEASES & ILLNESS

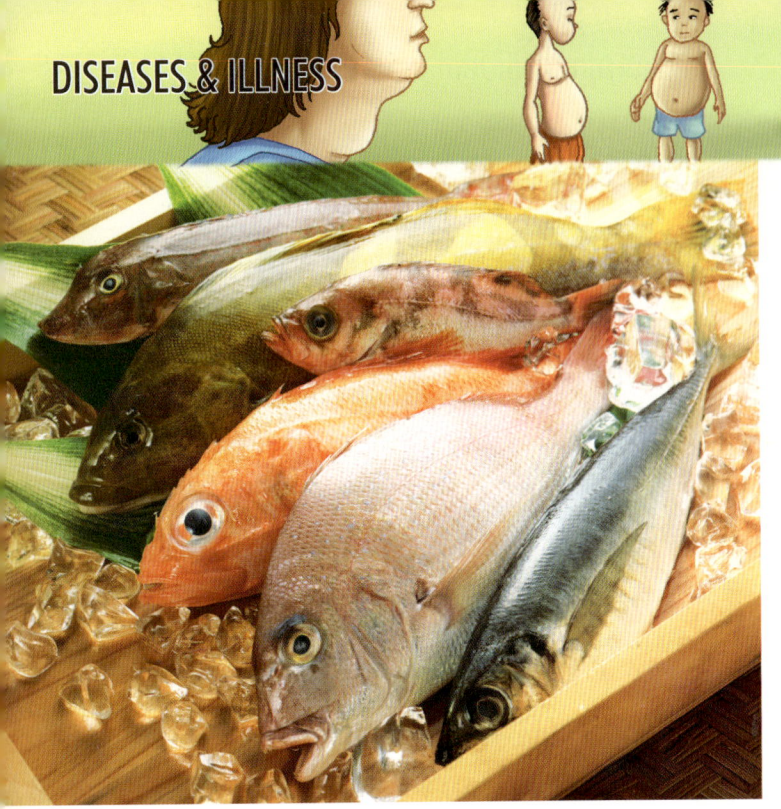

Food sources

The body does not produce iron, so it is important to get it from the diet. Poultry, lean meats, eggs, fish, beans and nuts are good sources of iron. It is also found in whole grain cereals, legumes, pulses, lentils, jaggery and fish. Vegetable sources include green leafy ones like turnip greens and cauliflower, while fruits include raisins, watermelons, currants and dried dates. Some iron is also absorbed by food cooked in iron vessels.

Iron is an essential trace element required for healthy blood, growth and vitality. Lack of iron or its absorption has serious consequences, so one must take iron rich food and keep the gastro-intestinal tract healthy to aid its absorption. Good sources are iron-rich fruits, which have their own acids and enzymes required for the digestion and assimilation of iron.

Diseases

Iron deficiency causes microcytic and hypochromic anaemia, a condition characterized by underdeveloped red blood cells that lack haemoglobin, thereby reducing the oxygen carrying capacity of red blood cells. But even before iron deficiency anaemia develops, people with poor iron status may experience a variety of symptoms including fatigue, weakness, loss of stamina, decreased ability to concentrate, increased susceptibility to infections, hair loss, dizziness, headaches, brittle nails, lethargy and depression.

Obesity can increase the chances of developing diseases such as type 2 diabetes and heart disease.

Types of nutritional deficiency diseases explained

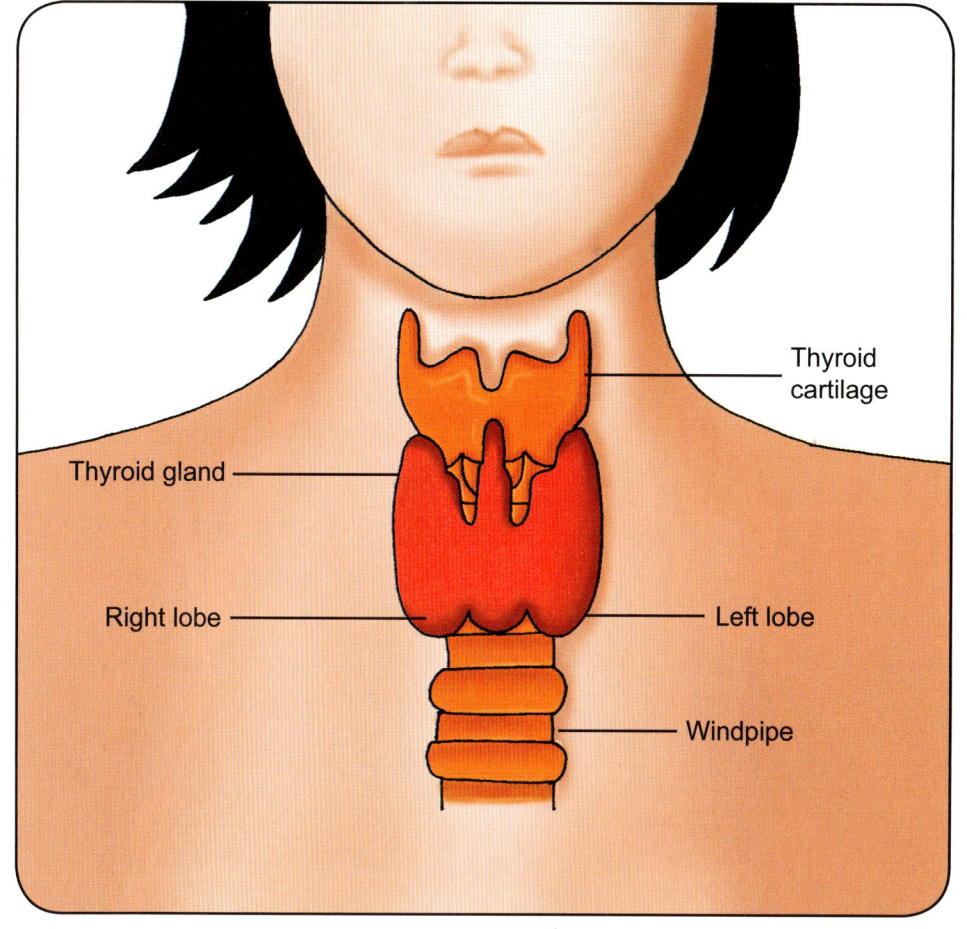

Iodine

Functions

Iodine is an essential mineral for the survival and sustenance of the human body, and a lack of iodine in the diet can lead to many iodine deficiency disorders (IDD). These are conditions that arise due to a lack of necessary iodine levels in the body and they can be cured by including healthy levels of iodine in one's diet.

The thyroid gland needs iodine to produce the body hormone thyroxine, which regulates the release of energy in the body. Iodine is mainly found in the thyroid glands and is an indispensable element for the body metabolism. Without it, a person gains weight and is fatigued. On the other hand, with hyperthyroid, a person loses weight and is hyperactive.

- Iodine prevents the development of simple goitre.
- Iodine plays a role in the development of hair, fingernails, skin and teeth.

In 2007, around 13 per cent of all deaths worldwide was caused by cancer. The branch of medicine related to cancer study and treatment is known as oncology.

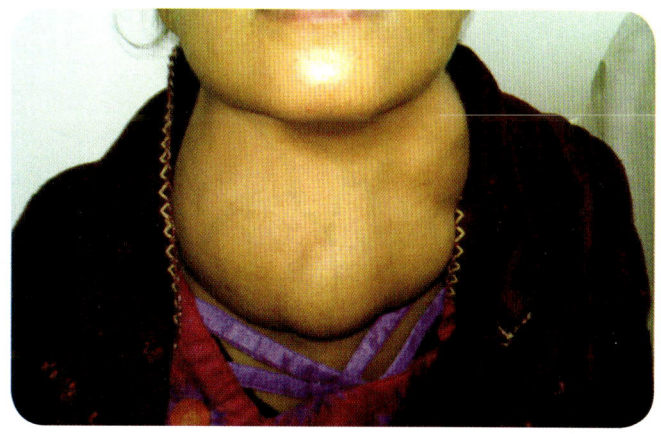

25

DISEASES & ILLNESS

- Its deficiency may also causes deafness and poor learning.
- Iodine deficiency or total loss will affect our mental and physical activity, obesity and hardening of blood vessels.
- A dietary lack of iodine may cause anaemia, tiredness, laziness, a slow pulse, low blood pressure and high blood cholesterol/triglyceride leading to heart disease.
- In children lack of iodine may lead to mental retardation, enlarged thyroid gland, defective speech and clumsy gait.

Food sources

Iodine is available in traces in water, food and common salts. Sea weeds and spongy shells are very rich in iodine. The best sources are sea fish, sea salt, green vegetables and leaves like spinach grown on iodine rich soil. The common sources are milk, meat and cereals. About 90 per cent of the iodine intake is obtained from the food consumed and the remainder from the water.

Diseases

- Iodine deficiency leads to enlargement of thyroid gland known as simple **goitre** which involves swelling of feet or toes, enlarged glands, excessive hunger, neuralgic pains in the heart, etc.

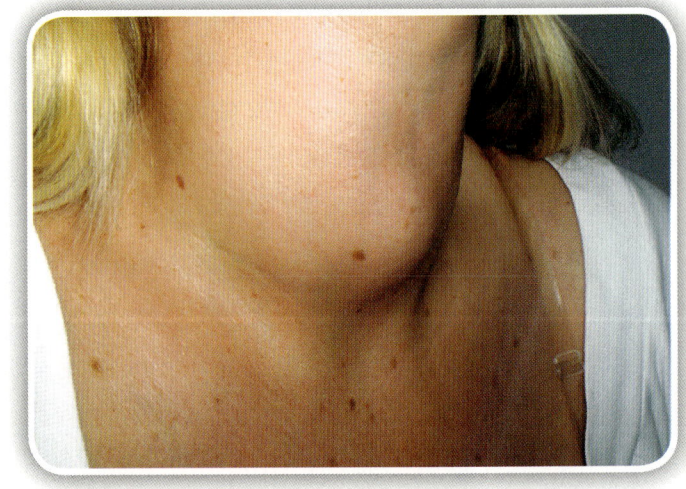

Index

A

amnesia 18
anaemia 8, 9, 16, 18, 20, 24, 26, 28, 29
ascorbic acid 19

B

B1/Thiamine 16
B2/Riboflavin 16
B3/Niacin 16
B5/ Pantothenic acid 16
B6/ Pyridoxine 16
B12 8, 9, 16, 17, 18
beriberi 8, 18, 30
biotin 16

C

calcium 7, 9, 14, 15, 21, 22, 27, 28, 29
calories 7, 9, 27, 30
carbohydrates 7, 16, 30
collagen 19

E

epidemics 3

F

fats 7, 16, 30
fibre 7
folic acid 16, 18

G

goitre 25, 26

H

haemoglobin 23, 24

I

iodine 7, 25, 26, 29
iron 7, 8, 9, 19, 23, 24, 27, 29

K

Kwashiorkor 27, 28

M

malnutrition 7, 27, 29
Marasmus 27, 28
medicine 4, 8, 25, 29,
mental illnesses 11
micro-organisms 5, 16
minerals 7, 14, 15, 27, 30
myoglobin 23

N

night blindness 13
Nosology 4
nutrients 7, 8, 9, 27, 29, 30
nutritional deficiency diseases 7, 29

O

osteomalacia 9, 22
osteopenia 22
osteoporosis 8, 15, 20, 22

P

Pathology 4

pellagra 8, 18
Primary PEM 27
Protein-energy malnutrition (PEM) 27, 29
proteins 7, 16, 30

R

red blood cells 8, 16, 22, 23, 24
retinol 12
rickets 8, 9, 15, 22

S

Scurvy 20, 30
Secondary PEM 27, 28
starvation 7, 9, 27, 29

T

thyroid gland 25, 26
thyroxine 25

V

Vitamin A 11, 12, 13, 21, 29, 30
Vitamin B complex 16
Vitamin C 19, 20, 21, 29, 30
Vitamin D 9, 14, 15, 21
vitamins 7, 16, 30

W

water 5, 7, 16, 19, 26
World Health Organization 8

Test Your MEMORY

1. What is a disease?

2. What is illness?

3. What are nutritional deficiency diseases?

4. Write briefly about the different types of illness.

5. Name the diseases caused by the lack of Vitamin A.

6. Name the diseases caused by the lack of Vitamin D.

7. What is Vitamin B Complex?

8. Name the food sources of Vitamin C.

9. Name the diseases caused by the lack of calcium.

10. Write about the functions of iron in our body.

11. Name the diseases caused by the lack of iodine.

12. What is protein energy malnutrition?

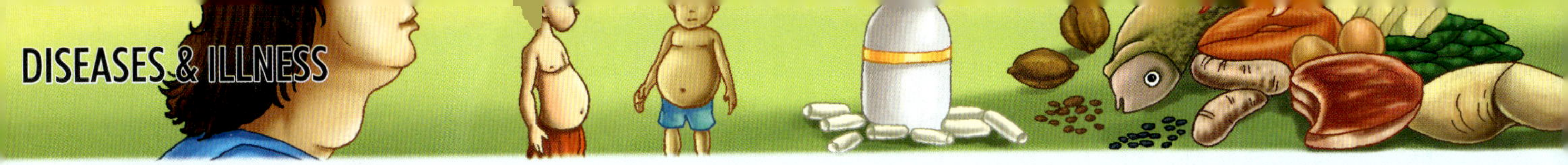

DISEASES & ILLNESS

Nutrition from the food you eat provides the energy and building materials you need to construct and maintain every organ and system. Virtually all food gives you energy, even when it does not give you nutrients. The amount of energy in food is measured in calories, the amount of heat produced when food is burned in your body cells. Food is the fuel on which your body runs. Without enough food, you don't have enough energy.

The body requires carbohydrates, fats, proteins, vitamins and minerals to maintain healthy organs, bones, muscles, nerves and to produce hormones and chemicals that are necessary for the proper function of organs. Vitamins and minerals are naturally occurring substances that are essential for the growth and function of the body. Vitamins and minerals are both necessary for normal chemical reactions (metabolism) in the body.

Vitamins and mineral supplements are important both in preventing deficiency states as well as in preventing diseases. Most diseases resulting from Vitamin deficiencies such as scurvy (Vitamin C deficiency), blindness (Vitamin A deficiency), and beriberi (thiamine deficiency) occur mainly in third-world countries.

Astonishing fact

Lack of sleep can affect your immune system and reduce your ability to fight infections.

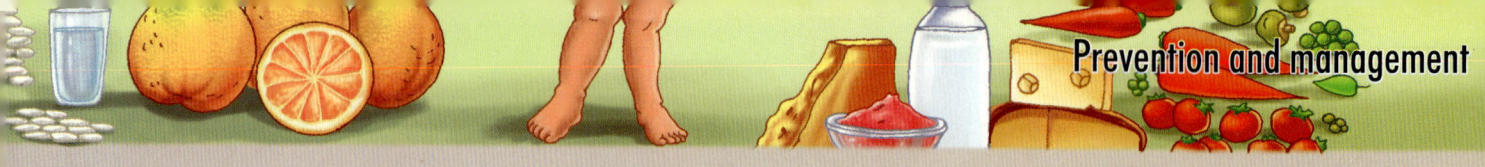

Prevention and management

Nutritional deficiency diseases result primarily from a diet that does not have enough of the nutrients that are essential to health or development. Another cause is that an individual may not be able to utilize properly the nutrients consumed in the diet. Deficiency diseases may result from a person's abnormally high metabolic needs for a nutrient or from some imbalance in the nutrients ingested. Certain drugs or medicines may also affect nutrient use. Deficiency diseases often result from insufficient food intake or a poorly balanced diet, but may also be caused by ill health (diarrhoea, parasitic infections, cancer, AIDS). The most severe deficiency disease is starvation, where there is marked weight reduction, loss of fat and other tissues, including from the liver and intestines. Most systems are affected, including the body's immune system. The skin and hair become dry. Diarrhoea often develops, and the sufferer may die of secondary infection. Nutritional deficiency contributes to much of the ill health in developing countries. The most important forms of malnutrition are protein-energy malnutrition, iodine deficiency disorders, vitamin A deficiency and nutritional anaemia.

Nutrients are the cornerstone of a healthy diet. If your diet doesn't include the proper nutrients, your health suffers. If you don't eat and drink nutritious food and beverages

- Your bones may bend or break (not enough calcium).
- Your gums may bleed (not enough Vitamin C).
- Your blood may not carry oxygen to every cell (not enough iron).

Astonishing fact

Food allergies are fairly common amongst adults and even more so among children. Around 2 per cent of adults and 8 per cent of children suffer from some type of food allergy where the immune system makes a mistake and thinks a certain food protein is dangerous and attacks it.

DISEASES & ILLNESS

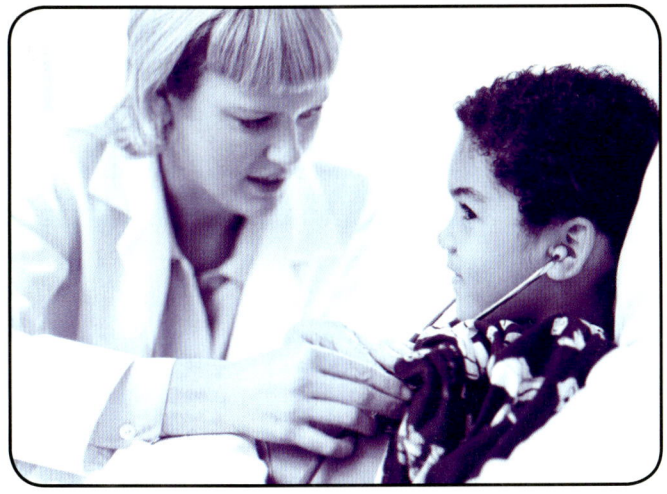

Secondary PEM symptoms range from mild to severe, and can alter the form or function of almost every organ in the body. The type and intensity of symptoms depend on the patient's prior nutritional status, the nature of the underlying disease, and the speed at which the PEM is progressing.

Mild, moderate and severe classifications for PEM have not been precisely defined, but patients who lose 10–20 per cent of their body weight without trying may have moderate PEM. This level of PEM is characterized by a weakened grip and inability to perform high-energy tasks.

Losing 20 per cent of body weight or more is generally classified as severe PEM. Children with this condition cannot eat normal-sized meals. They have slow heart rates and low blood pressure and body temperatures. Other symptoms of severe secondary PEM include baggy, wrinkled skin, constipation, dry, thin, or brittle hair, lethargy, pressure sores and other skin lesions.

Children suffering from kwashiorkor often have extremely thin arms and legs, but liver enlargement and ascites (abnormal accumulation of fluid) can distend the abdomen and disguise weight loss. Hair may turn red or yellow. Anaemia, diarrhoea, fluid and electrolyte disorders are common. The body's immune system is often weakened, behavioural development is slow and mental retardation may occur. Children may grow to normal height but are abnormally thin.

Profound weakness accompanies severe marasmus. Since the body breaks down its own tissue to use for energy, children with this condition lose all their body fat and muscle strength, and acquire a skeletal appearance most noticeable in the hands and in the temporal muscle in front of and above each ear. Children with marasmus are small for their age. Since their immune systems are weakened, they suffer from frequent infections. Other symptoms include loss of appetite, diarrhoea, skin that is dry and baggy, sparse hair that is dull brown or reddish yellow, mental retardation, behavioural retardation, low body temperature (hypothermia) and slow pulse and breathing rates.

Astonishing fact

Eggs contain the highest quality food protein known. All parts of an egg are edible, including the shell which has high calcium content.

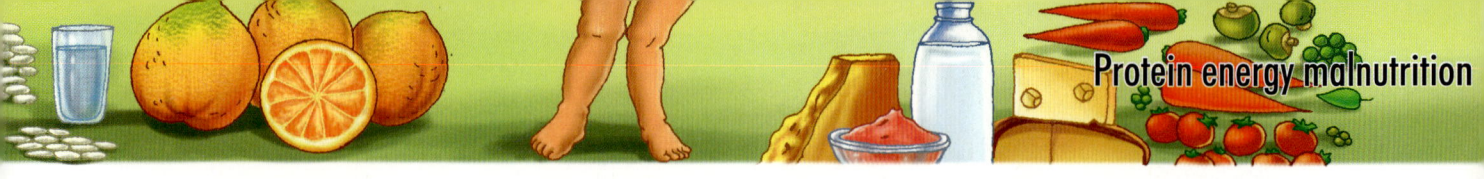

Protein energy malnutrition

Protein-energy malnutrition (PEM) is a potentially fatal body-depletion disorder. It is the leading cause of death in children in developing countries.

PEM is also referred to as protein-calorie malnutrition. It develops in children whose consumption of protein and energy (measured by calories) is insufficient to satisfy their nutritional needs. While pure protein deficiency can occur when a person's diet provides enough energy but lacks an adequate amount of protein, in most cases deficiency will exist in both total calorie and protein intake. PEM may also occur in children with illnesses that leave them unable to absorb vital nutrients or convert them to the energy essential for healthy tissue formation and organ function.

Primary PEM results from a diet that lacks sufficient sources of protein. Secondary PEM is more common in the United States, where it usually occurs as a complication of AIDS, cancer, chronic kidney failure, inflammatory bowel disease and other illnesses that impair the body's ability to absorb or use nutrients or to compensate for nutrient losses. PEM can develop gradually in a child who has a chronic illness or experiences chronic semi-starvation. It may appear suddenly in a patient who has an acute illness.

Kwashiorkor, also called wet protein-energy malnutrition, is a form of PEM characterized primarily by protein deficiency. This condition usually appears at about the age of 12 months when breast-feeding is discontinued, but it can develop at any time during a child's formative years. It causes fluid retention (edema); dry, peeling skin and hair discoloration.

Marasmus, a PEM disorder, is caused by total calorie/energy depletion rather than primarily protein calorie/energy depletion. Marasmus is characterized by stunted growth and wasting of muscle and tissue. Marasmus usually develops between the ages of six months and one year in children who have been weaned from breast milk or who suffer from weakening conditions such as chronic diarrhoea.

Astonishing fact
Minerals constitute 4 per cent of our body weight. Minerals include calcium, iron and sodium.